Baskets
to appliqué

kay mackenzie

Special thanks

To so many people. No one gets anywhere alone. My husband, Dana Mackenzie, who has no issues with me spending my time quilting, writing, and illustrating instead of practicing domestic skills. Willie the papillon (the real quilt puppy) for keeping me company in the studio and pre-approving all of my quilts. Appliqué friends Pam Crooks and Janet Locey for taking designs on paper and working their usual magic with fabric.

"Work toward perfection, remembering all the while that it cannot be achieved."
—Quilt Puppy motto

Contents

Introduction	3
Basket Designs	4–23
Photo Gallery	17–20
Sixteen Baskets Quilt	24–26
Kay's Hand Appliqué Tips	27–35
The Particulars	36

On the cover

Sixteen Baskets (detail)
Hand appliquéd and hand quilted by Kay Mackenzie
Photo on page 19

ISBN-13: 978-0-9725852-5-5
ISBN-10: 0-9725852-5-7
©Baskets to Appliqué
©2006 Kay Mackenzie. All rights reserved. Printed and bound in the U.S.A. First Printing.

Gentle quilter, please note that the right to copy and distribute belongs to the copyright holder. Owners of this book may make copies of the designs for ease of use in their personal projects. Copying any part of this book in any manner to give away or to sell without permission is against copyright law. The designs are intended primarily for personal projects, including gifts. Nonprofit fund-raising efforts using the designs are welcome; please contact the publisher first. Contact the publisher for any commercial use of the designs. The information herein is presented in good faith. However, since the publisher has no control over users' materials, procedures, or skills, no warranty or guarantee of results can be given.

Quilt Puppy
Publications & Designs

P.O. Box 1241
Aptos, California 95001
www.quiltpuppy.com

For additional copies of this book, ask at your favorite quilt shop or visit www.quiltpuppy.com.

Greetings appliqué enthusiasts!

Your favorite method

There are quite a few ways to appliqué, and many variations within broad categories of technique. Appliquérs naturally gravitate toward the methods that work for them and give them personal satisfaction in their results. It's all good! This little book provides designs for your appliqué pleasure using your methods and your own creative instincts.

Whether your style is raw-edge, prepared-edge, or needle-turn, fusing or stitching, by hand or machine —pick your favorite baskets and fill them with fun!

Your quilt

Make one block or many. Make them larger or smaller. Mix and match them, choose your favorites and put them together, or sprinkle a few into your next project. The quilts you make will celebrate your own style and personality.

Hand appliqué

The method I enjoy most is hand appliqué. Beginning on page 27 I've included my own personal tips for the way I work, which you may find useful if you appliqué by hand as well or would like to read more about it. With each design I've also included bits of construction information for working by hand. Notes about particular blocks refer to the **Sixteen Baskets** quilt on page 19.

Design elements

There are many possibilities for personalizing the baskets. Several of the designs include decorative elements that are optional. You may prefer to let a special fabric do the work instead. Change what's in a particular basket for something else, or choose a different flower. Make your baskets to suit your own creative eye. In the photo gallery you'll see just some of the possibilities for varying the designs.

Sizing

The patterns as printed are sized for an 8" finished block. The same size could go on a 9" or 10" block if you'd like more space around the motifs. To reduce or enlarge the patterns themselves, photocopy according to the following percentages:

    6" block — 75%
    9" block — 112.5%
    10" block — 125%
    12" block — 150%

To enlarge, fold the pattern in halves or in quarters, enlarge each section by the same percentage, then trim and tape the sections together.

Orientation

Horizontal and vertical centering marks are given for each design.

To reflect a block, choose a mirror-image option on a photocopy machine, or trace the design onto tracing paper with a heavy marker and flip it over.

Strips, stems, or vines

There is no right or wrong for the width of the stems in these designs. No matter how a design appears, you may choose to embroider them, use your favorite skinny stem technique, or make ¼" stems. On page 29 I describe the method that I use for making quick ¼" strips, stems, or vines, as well as a variation for making skinny ones.

Fine details

Fine details can be accomplished using embroidery, fabric pen, beads, buttons, or the technique of your choice. Throughout the pages of the designs you'll find information of how I added fine details to the blocks in **Sixteen Baskets**.

Straight lines

...can be the most challenging to appliqué by hand. To achieve the diamonds, cut templates out of stiff paper. Baste the margins of the fabric over the templates and press, trimming excess fabric from the narrow points. After stitching, remove the basting and open the background fabric to remove the templates.

Baskets *to appliqué*

Flowers in nature

...are not perfect, and that is part of their beauty. The many small petals of these daisies may wave to a slightly different wind than what is shown here without affecting the success of the block.

My new favorite way of embroidering tendril-thin stems is to couch a full six-strand length of embroidery thread in place. I used one strand of a lighter shade for the couching stitches.

Curved strips

...are easy these days with the help of a really cool gadget. See page 29 for tips on how to make quick bias strips that already have the edges turned for you and can even be fused in place for stitching.

This design is a nod to a traditional basket often seen in Baltimore Album style quilts, as is the woven basket, opposite.

This is another block based on tradition. You can also use just the outline to make a basket. See page 20 for an example.

Straight strips

...are easy with the same gadget that makes bias strips. See page 29 for tips on how to make quick straight strips that already have the edges turned. Making them fusible is a recommended technique for this block.

Lightly trace the placement of the woven strips onto the background fabric. Place the block on a pinnable surface. Using the marked lines and referring to the pattern, weave the strips in an over-and-under fashion, pinning the ends. After all raw edges are covered with the outer strips and you are satisfied with the arrangement, fuse or baste in place.

Skinny stems

...are only a little more challenging than their wider counterparts. See page 29 for information on how I make skinny stems using a little ingenuity... and a glue stick.

I foundation-pieced the main body of the basket, and then used it as a prepared element for appliqué.

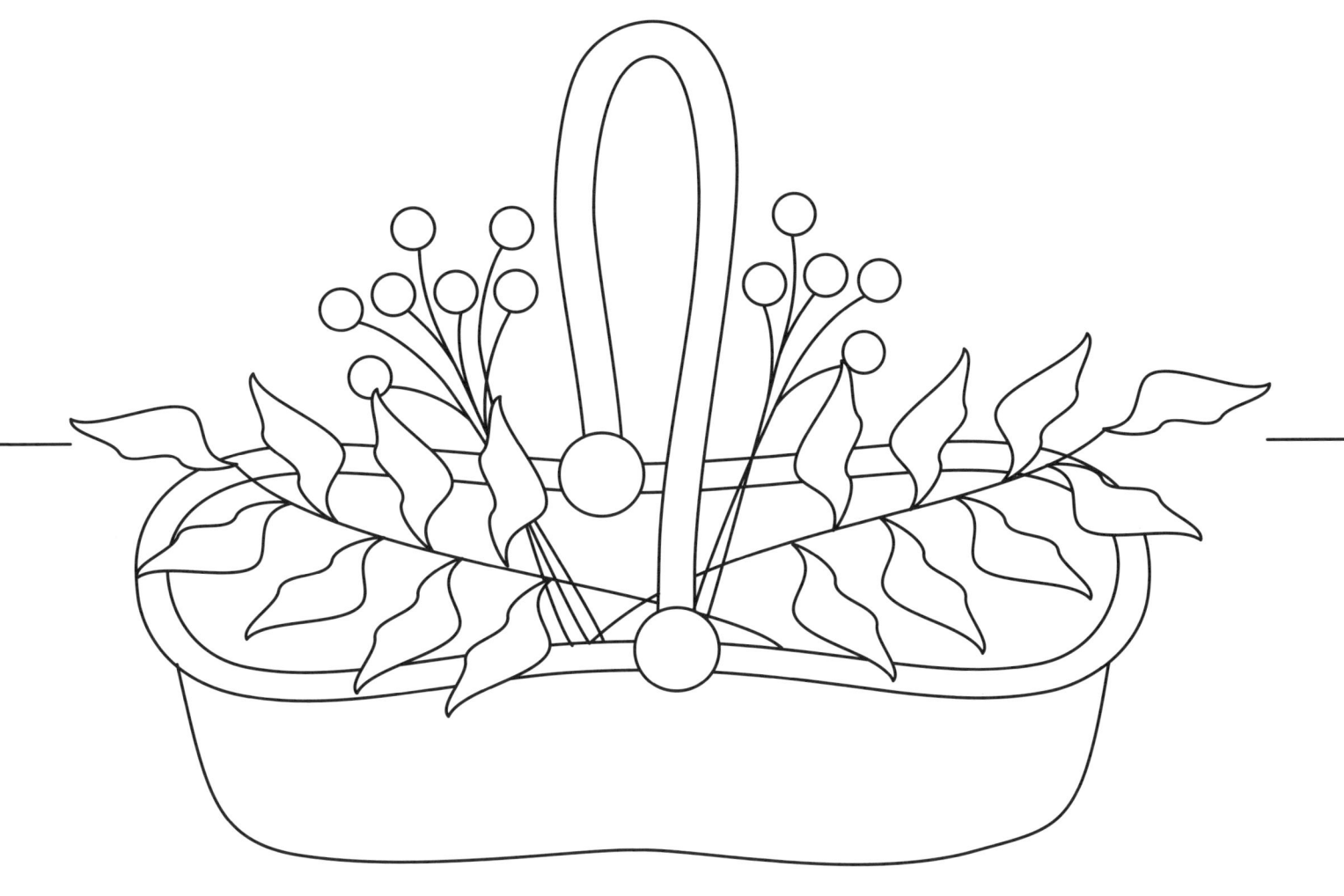

Tiny elements

...like the leaves and berries in this herb basket are candidates for fusing and machine stitching. In a larger block size, they become more approachable for hand appliqué.

For the tendril-thin stems, I couched a full six-strand length of embroidery thread in place, using one strand of a lighter shade.

Fine details

...such as the features of this well-behaved (but perhaps mischief-minded) cat can be accomplished using embroidery, fabric pen, beads, buttons, or the technique of your choice.

I embroidered the face, as well as the individual strands of knitting yarn. The knitting needles can be made with skinny straight strips (see page 29). Round off the ends of the heads while stitching.

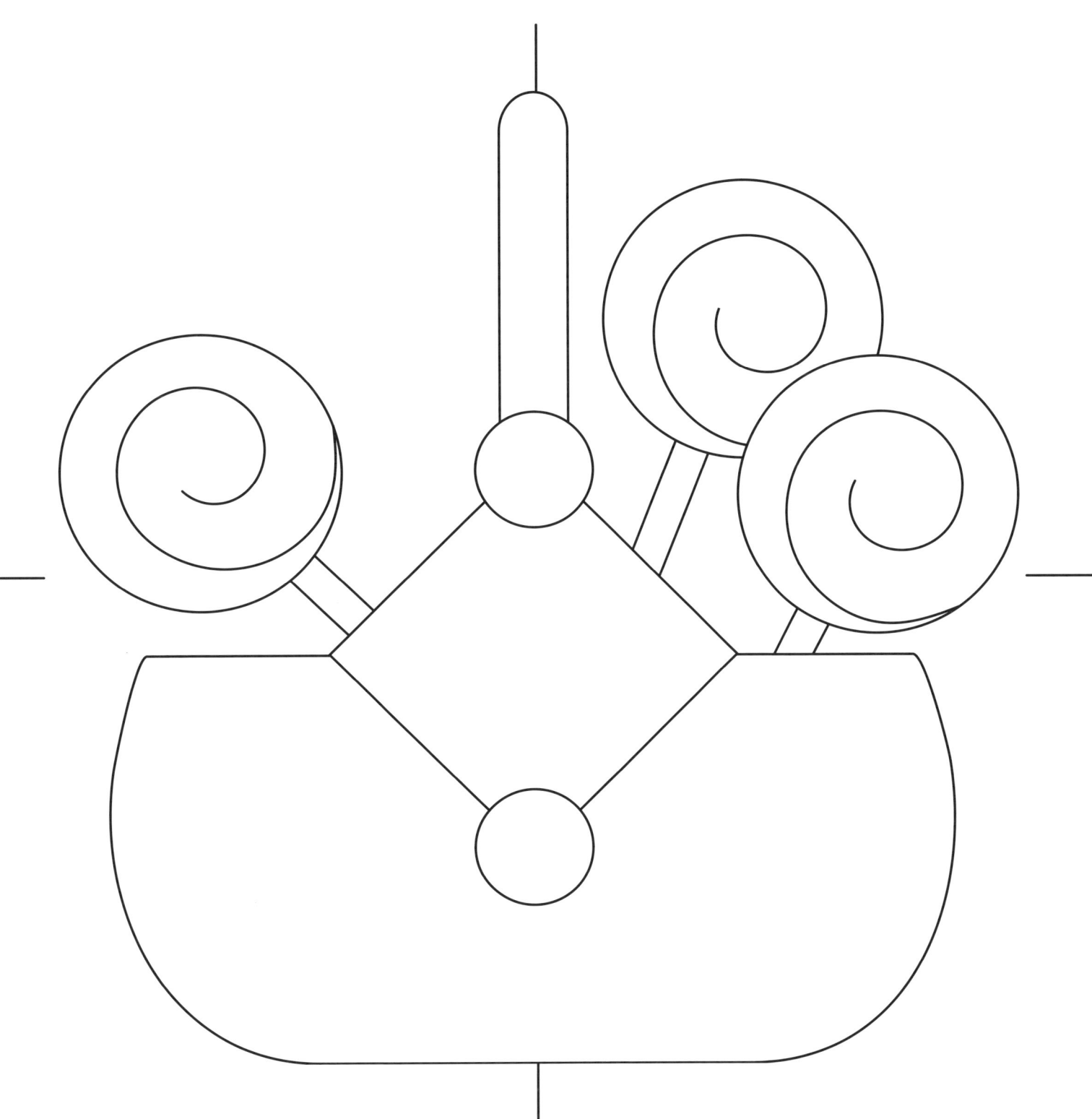

Wide expanses

...are perfect opportunities to use fabrics that are the most dear to your heart. This and the sewing basket on the following page give you lots of room for fabric showcase.

This block also allows you to pull out several items from your appliqué bag of tricks, including straight lines (page 4), straight strips (page 29) and fine details. Embroider, ink, or quilt the swirls into the lollipops.

Illusions of perspective

...can be very small details that contribute to the look of depth in a design. In this sewing basket we see very small parts of the inside of the basket. The tracing-paper overlay (page 28), or another successful placement method is crucial for getting these small bits in the proper places.

The open expanse of this basket provides the perfect opportunity to feature a special fabric.

I used a fabric pen to mark the swirls that contribute to the rolled look of the fat quarters.

The basics

...of appliqué include good techniques for points and notches, as seen in the leaves and the five-petal posies. See pages 33–34 for tips on these techniques, plus step-by-step illustrations.

This block also presents the opportunity to use bias strips, straight strips, and skinny strips. See page 29.

Baskets *to appliqué*

Stitching order

...is often dictated by the design. In this case, the inside back of the basket has to go down first, then the stems, then the front of the basket. Leave extra length on the ends of the stems until you are certain that all raw edges will be covered.

For the 8" block size, I fused and machine-stitched my butterfly. In a larger size, it could be more easily stitched by hand.

Stitching order

...is sometimes not dictated by the design, but can be open to interpretation. In this instance, the base of the basket can go over or under the body, and the body can go over or under the inside. When I made my basket, I put the body over the base, and the inside over the body, as this was an easier stitching situation. It still looks like the inside.

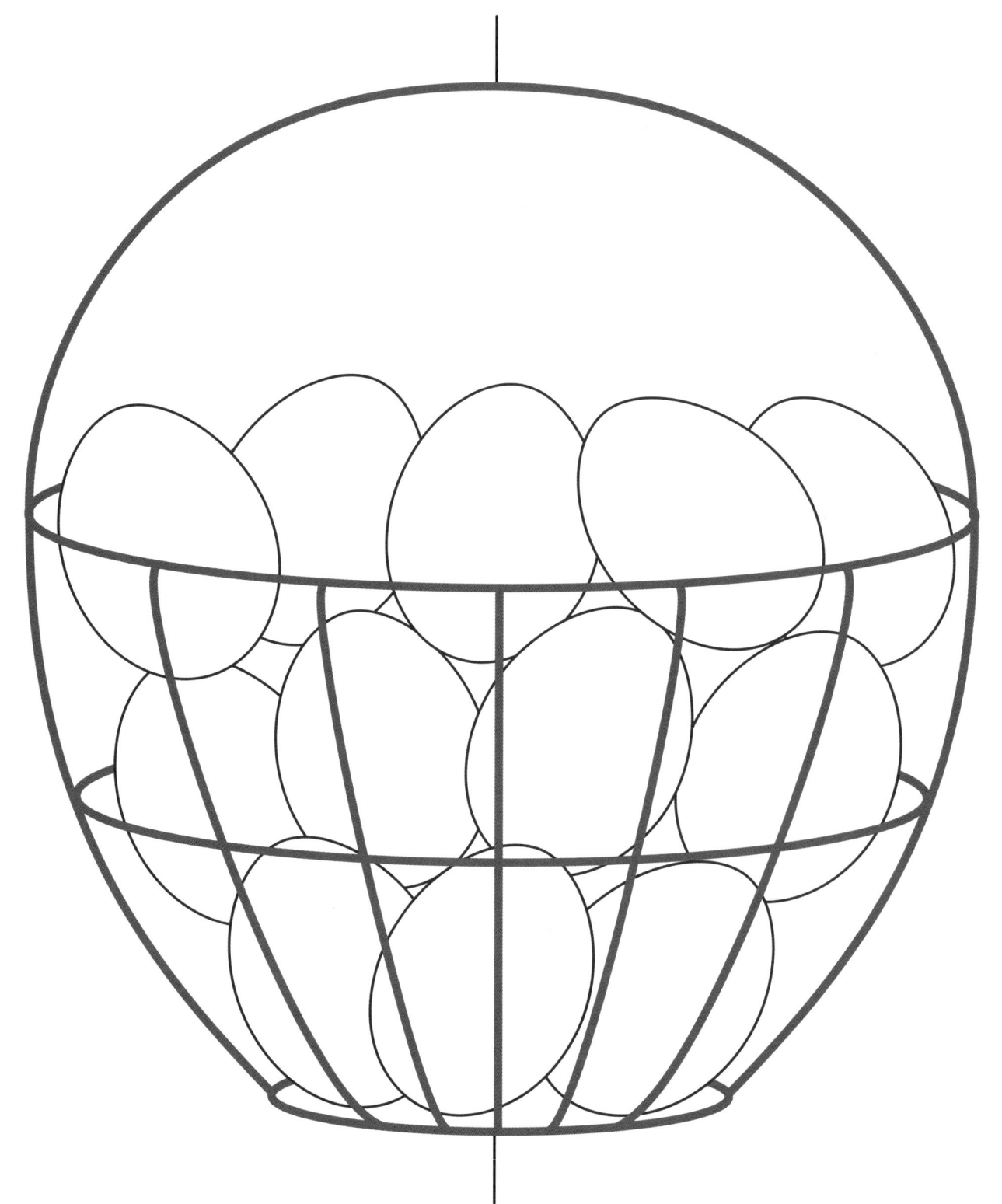

Unusual situations

...provide excellent challenges for putting on your thinking cap. When I made my egg basket, I used the bias skinny strip technique described on page 29, and when it came time to round the turn at the sides, I allowed the strips to go upside down. In these very short lengths, the raw edges are not distinguishable.

I released a few stitches of the eggs, inserted the ends of the strips, and restitched.

Janet, the master of machines, used another approach. She free-motion-embroidered the basket over marked lines. See page 20 for her version.

Broderie Perse

Here's a really fun and easy variation. I cut a bouquet from a beautiful floral print and put it in the ivy basket (page 22), omitting the handle. I used fusible web and a small machine blanket stitch.

Black Magic

Pam Crooks created a stunning effect using glowing batiks on a black background.

Notice the great mileage she got out of the striped fabric in the daisy basket.

These blooming baskets are fused and machine-stitched.

Cut Flowers

machine appliquéd by Kay
28" x 28"

This dramatic four-block wall quilt employs a limited palette pulled from the floral border fabric.

Notice the variations in two of the designs. The knitting basket (page 10) now holds roses. The posy basket (page 13) is mirror-imaged and the simplified triangular section is adorned with a heart.

Sixteen Baskets

by Kay Mackenzie
hand appliquéd and hand quilted by Kay
38" x 38"

I used warm browns, soldier blue, and a variety of floral colors for my basket collection. Instructions begin on page 24 for this sampler quilt with diamond setting stones and classic dogtooth border.

Change it up

From psychedelic to sophisticated, retro to vintage, classic to country, the choice of fabrics can create the look and feel you like.

You can change what's in the baskets. See how the sewing basket, formerly stuffed with fat quarters, has become a knitting basket full of yarn. If you'd like to do that, the lollipop is the same size as the ball of yarn and can be used as a template. Arrange the yarn and knitting needles as desired.

I made a groovy daisy basket, and the woven basket is now solid to show off a favorite elegant fabric.

Make the designs as they are, or modify, simplify, change them to suit your mind's eye. Use your own preferred methods, or make up a new one. There's no right or wrong when the result is pleasing to you.

The Main Ingredient

Janet Locey made the appetizing baskets below. To create her egg basket, she used free-motion machine embroidery with a heavy black thread, stitching over marked lines after appliquéing the eggs.

A little embroidery

...can be an effective solution. I knew there had to be a way to embroider the chain for this hanging basket, and sure enough, when I looked it up in a reference book of basic stitches, it turned out to be the "braid stitch," which is a series of "lazy daisy" stitches.

I practiced on a piece of scrap fabric, then went for it. I used perle cotton, and afterwards couched the links in place with regular thread to make sure they would maintain an open appearance.

Removing the background

...is something to think about if you are a hand quilter. If the background fabric is not removed behind the body of this basket, the hand quilter will have an extra layer to quilt through.

One way to approach this is to appliqué the ivy leaf onto the basket first, then appliqué the basket as a prepared element onto the background fabric. This leaves the background free for trimming away. The other is to appliqué the basket, trim away the background, then add the leaf and stem.

Choices

...are available in appliqué. Often there is no right or wrong way to render a design. You can appliqué each petal of the primrose individually, or treat each shape as a whole. In my version, I chose to appliqué the outer flower shape as one piece, then applied each inner petal individually.

For the handle, I chose not to use bias strips, and instead used freezer-paper templates.

The bird's beak is embroidered, and his eye is a French knot. His feet are silk ribbon, sewn down with a running stitch and scrunched up a bit for his feet.

Sixteen Baskets 38" x 38"

Here's a sampler quilt to show off your entire basket collection. The diamond setting stones and the dogtooth border add even more fun. Photo on page 19.

Fabric requirements

Background & outer borders ... 1½ yards
Baskets .... assorted scraps
                                              or fabrics as desired
Inner borders, dogtooth appliqué,
diamonds .... ½ yard

- Blocks in this quilt are 8" finished size. Background squares will be cut oversized at first, then trimmed after appliqué is complete.

- FYI: Backing will require 1¼ yards.

- For the dogtooth border, you'll need a marking implement that is easily removed, such as a white chalk pencil.

Cut these things

Background squares .... (16) 9" squares
Outer borders .... (4) 2¾" x width of fabric

Inner borders
& dogtooth appliqué ....(8) 1½" x width of fabric
Diamonds (hand appliqué) .. (9) 1½" squares*

*For machine appliqué, prepare (9) 1" squares with fusible product on outer edges only.

Instructions

Using your favorite method, appliqué baskets to background squares. Trim blocks to 8½". Lay out blocks as desired. Sew each row together.

—Row 1

—Row 2

In odd rows, press seam allowances to one side.
In even rows, press toward opposite side.
Nestling seams, sew rows together and press.

Quilt top should now measure 32½" x 32½".

Diamonds

Next add the diamonds over each seam intersection.

Hand appliqué: Cut (9) 1" square templates out of stiff paper (the little cards that fall out of quilting magazines are perfect).

Place the templates behind the diamond fabric squares. Turn the margins over the papers and baste. Press with a dry iron.

Aligning the corners with the seams on all four sides, baste the diamonds in place on the quilt top over each four-block intersection. Appliqué. Remove all basting stitches. The templates will be removed later.

Machine appliqué: Fuse in place, with fusible product applied to outer edges of diamonds only. To avoid pressing an impression of the seam into the diamond, use the tip of the iron on the outer edges only. Stitch.

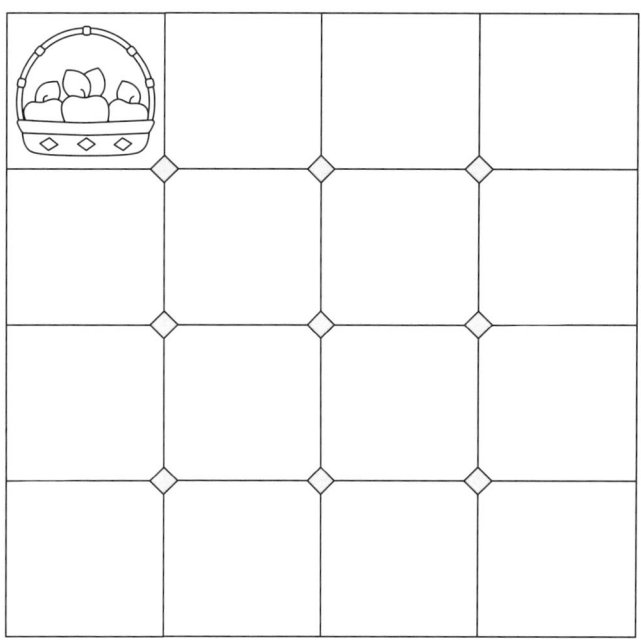

An appliquér's mitered border

This is the way I sew mitered borders—from the top, where I can see what I'm doing.

Sew each inner border strip to an outer border strip. Press seam allowances toward inner borders. Fold each strip set in half lengthwise and crease.

Match centers with the quilt top. With the inner borders toward the quilt, sew a strip set to each side, leaving ¼" free at each end of the seams and securing the starting and stopping points with backstitching. Press seam allowances toward inner borders. The borders will be longer than the quilt top. That's good.

Place quilt on the ironing board. Fold one border under at a 45° angle so that it lines up exactly with its neighbor underneath. Use your ruler to check the angle of the miter and its 45° relationship to the square corner block. When all is satisfactory, press and then carefully baste in place without shifting the fabric. Appliqué the miter, using threads to match the fabrics. Remove basting stitches.

Complete all four corners in this manner. After a final check that all corners are square and correct, trim off excess border ends, leaving a ¼" seam allowance. Press seams open.

Remember to leave ¼" free at each end of the seams when sewing the borders to the quilt. Backstitch at the starting and stopping points.

The side border is folded under at a 45° angle and is resting on the top border, lined up exactly so that the seams and edges meet in a perfect miter.

Dogtooth border

The hand-stitched dogtooth border is a classic addition to an appliqué quilt. The template provided here is sized specifically for this quilt, and includes an extra ¼" on the outer edge that can be trimmed away if desired when ready to bind the finished quilt. The cut width given for the outer borders also includes this extra ¼".

Photocopy or trace the template onto paper. Reinforce by laminating or applying clear packing tape to both sides. Cut out the template on the outer lines. Or, make a plastic or cardboard template.

Baste the outer edges of the dogtooth strips to the outer borders of the quilt, raw edges together. Place the template on a strip, aligning outer edges, and mark 22 teeth on each border. The first and last tooth on each end should fall exactly on a miter line.

Full-size template. Mark 22 teeth across each border strip between miter lines.

When each side is correctly marked, begin stitching with the second tooth on any side. Trim away excess fabric between points as you go, leaving a turn-under margin. The template and fabric strip are sized so that there is just the right amount of margin at the top of each tooth for a nice point. When you reach the corner, appliqué the last tooth over the first tooth of the next border to form a straight line, as shown. Continue trimming and stitching until all four borders are complete.

Finishing

Just before layering, carefully trim away seam intersections of background fabric under diamond setting stones, leaving about ¼" inside stitching line. Remove templates.

Layer, baste, quilt as desired, bind, and label your appliqué basket quilt.

Kay's hand appliqué tips

Even within the particular method of appliqué known as "traditional needle-turn," there are many approaches and variations. Given here are some notes about the strategies that I employ, which may prove useful if you are interested in hand appliqué.

Fabric selection

Choose 100% cotton fabrics of a medium weight and a soft, pliable hand. Fabrics containing polyester have "spring" and will resist the creasing and turning of the margins. Too-thin or loosely woven fabrics will ravel easily and wear out more quickly. Fabrics found in independent quilt shops are generally of the highest quality and easiest to work with.

Prints hide stitches better than solid fabrics. If you'd like to achieve the overall look of solid colors, you can use tone-on-tone prints for added depth and glow. If you're happy with your stitching, don't hesitate to use solids if they give you the look you're after.

Fabric preparation

Some quilters prefer not to wash their fabrics. I like the feel of clean fabric, so I wash it as soon as I get it.

Cut the background fabric a little larger than the unfinished size. For an 8" block (8½" unfinished), cut the background at least 9" square. After the block is completed, you will trim it to the unfinished size.

To create positioning marks, fold the background fabric in quarters and crease the outer edges. You can add small pencil marks in the creases at the very edges of the fabric. Mark each stem, strip, or vine with one central line. No further marking is needed. A tissue overlay will serve as a placement guide.

Tools and notions

Use sharp pointy hand scissors, not big shears. My favorite size is 5"; other quilters use smaller embroidery scissors.

Use fine thread that matches the piece being appliquéd (not the background). I use 50-weight cotton two-ply machine-embroidery thread. Others use 50-weight three-ply or 60-weight thread, and still others swear by very fine silk thread. The important thing is to use a fine thread in a natural material. Avoid the polyester thread that comes on the skinny spools. It is not meant for hand sewing.

Use appliqué needles. Yes, even if you have trouble threading them. No. 11 straw or milliner's needles (same thing) or No. 11 sharps are excellent choices. Whatever the brand or number, the important thing is that it's a skinny needle that glides through fabric easily without resistance.

A threading tip

Instead of holding the needle in midair and trying to poke the thread though the eye, try this method.

Cut a fresh end of the thread. Pinch the end between your thumb and forefinger. Slowly open up the tips of thumb and forefinger until the end of the thread is just visible. With the other hand, bring the eye of the needle down over the thread.

Many who swear they cannot thread a needle succeed on the very first try when shown this strategy.

Vision

If you wear glasses, making sure that your prescription is up-to-date can be very important in getting good appliqué results.

I never needed glasses, but at a certain age I had to admit that I found myself in a situation. Does this sound at all familiar? You can't see the grain of the fabric; you can't find the eye of the needle; you're holding your quilting magazine at arm's length. Gentle quilter, it's time to go to the drugstore and get some of those groovy granny glasses. Pick up a pill bottle and try on pairs until you can read the teeny-tiny writing. Presbyopia, otherwise known as "over-forty eyes," is a natural process that causes a stiffening in the eyes' focusing mechanism, making it difficult to see small things close up. Non-prescription reading glasses magnify the small things and add back details to your vision that you may not have noticed were missing for awhile. This is important for your good appliqué results.

Lighting

Good lighting goes hand-in-hand with good vision for supporting the success of your appliqué efforts.

If your sewing light is just adequate, make a special effort to arrange for more lighting or lighting that is better directed on your work.

Many quilters enjoy having the compact-fluorescent type of lights, either portable models or goose-neck floor lamps. I like incandescent lighting better. Choose the type of light that makes you feel most comfortable and invest in a lamp for your work area that can be redirected as needed to illuminate your appliqué. A second lamp for taking along to workshops and retreats is very nice to have. Don't forget to pack an extra bulb.

Pattern preparation

Select or design your appliqué pattern. On the outer edges of the pattern, mark the vertical and horizontal centers if not already provided. These marks will correspond to the creases on the background fabric.

Study the pattern to decide the stitching order of the pieces (aka motifs). Begin with pieces that are partially behind other pieces, and build to the front. It's often helpful to number the pieces in sequence on the pattern. You can also make note of the fabric or color you've assigned.

I use a tissue overlay as a placement guide. To create the overlay, trace the entire pattern onto tracing paper. A pencil is fine for this. Also transfer the centering marks. You won't need the numbers or the color notes on the overlay.

Larger sizes of tracing paper are available at stationery or art-supply stores. You can also tape together sheets of tracing paper if needed for larger patterns.

Template preparation

For motifs other than stems or vines, I use freezer-paper templates. This means no marking on the fabrics is needed. The templates are ironed onto the front of the fabric. You can appliqué with the freezer paper still in place, or you can remove it for a more traditional needle-turn technique. More on that later.

From the original pattern, trace each appliqué piece individually onto the paper side of the freezer paper. To denote a portion of a piece that is overlapped by another piece, use a dashed line. Transfer the numbers and color notes as well.

For multiples of the same shape, like leaves, I usually make a template for each. Some quilters layer and cut multiple templates at once, but you may find more accuracy in tracing and cutting each one individually.

Cut out each template on the drawn line. Where there is a dashed line, cut slightly to the outside of it (so you can see that it's a dashed line).

Stems or vines

Usually, when an appliqué project calls for stems or vines, I reach for my trusty green gadget—the original Clover® ¼" bias-tape maker. Here are some tips for how I get it to work easily for me.

Cut the bias strip ⅝" wide. Cut the top of the strip at an angle upward to the left (it seems to feed through better this way).

Right side of fabric

Cut on bias

⅝" wide

Poke the strip right-side-up into the wider end of the gadget until you can see the fabric in the slot on top. Use the tip of a pin to pull the strip through the slot until it sticks out at the narrow end. Pin the strip to the ironing board. Be sure to use a glass-head pin, so you don't have to worry about melting a plastic pin.

Using a hot iron and plenty of steam, pull the gadget along the strip with one smooth, fairly rapid motion, following it closely with the iron. Don't stop part-way through, or try to back up. Smoothness is key.

Important: Hold your iron so that the steam vents are not directed at your fingers.

Skinny stems

You can go this one further to create skinny stems that are about ⅛" wide. You'll need the gadget plus a fresh fabric glue stick and a wet towel to wipe your fingers on.

Make a ¼" bias stem as described. Then open out one fold and press it back flat. You will still be able to see the crease. Trim off the fabric just outside the crease.

Now apply glue to the wrong side of the strip and fold and pinch the raw edge back over to the center. It should stick with cheerful obedience. If it doesn't work well for you the first time, use a little more glue or make sure the glue stick is fresh.

If you would prefer to skip the gluing, you can appliqué the folded edge first, then tuck under the raw edge on the other side as you stitch.

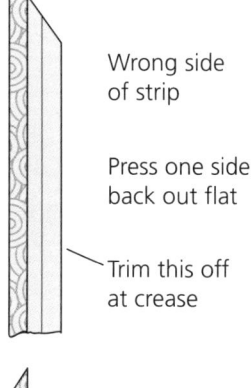

Wrong side of strip

Press one side back out flat

Trim this off at crease

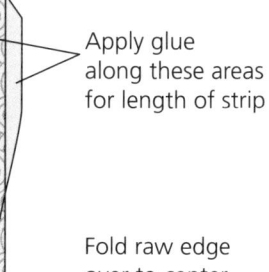

Apply glue along these areas for length of strip

Fold raw edge over to center

Making them fusible

You can make bias or straight strips fusible by applying thin strips of paper-backed fusible web. I do this as a second step. The product comes on a roll and can be found alongside the bias tape makers. I usually cut the strips of fusible in half lengthwise, so that there is only a tiny amount applied in the center of the strip. This is enough to keep the stems or vines secure for stitching.

Straight strips

For ¼" straight strips, cut the strips on the straight grain instead of on the bias, and cut them only ½" wide. Then use the gadget the same way.

Motif preparation

With a dry iron, not overly hot, press the templates shiny-side-down onto the right side of the motif fabrics, leaving at least ½" between templates. Press just long enough for the freezer paper to adhere. A piece of cardboard underneath the fabric helps create a better bond. For most pieces, the grain of the fabric is not important. A bias edge is actually easier to appliqué than a straight-grain edge. For jumbo-size pieces, it's a good idea to orient the templates so that the motif's grain lines match the background fabric's.

Allow fabric and templates to cool briefly. Then, handling as little as possible, cut the motif area apart from the main body of the fabric. Sit down and cut the motifs apart. Then pick up each motif and trim carefully in preparation for appliquéing.

A ¼" margin is actually too much for most appliqué pieces. This amount creates bulk and encourages bumps and blunt-ended points. Leave only about 3/16" margin, even 1/8" for very small pieces. This makes some quilters nervous, but fine work is achieved through this closer trim. Leave extra margin on the dashed-line portions that will be overlapped by other pieces.

Clipping

In notches, clip almost to the template with the tip of your scissors. Fairly steep inside curves will need a series of shallow clips. Do not clip outer curves.

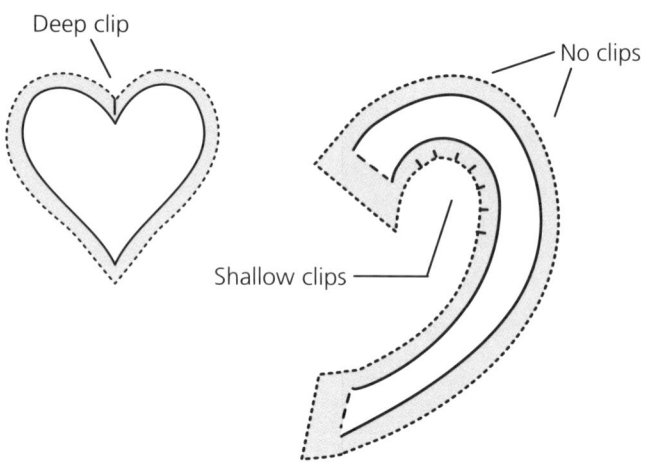

Keep your motifs in a little box or a file folder. Leave the templates on and handle them as little as possible until ready to sew.

Decision time

This is the point at which you'll decide whether to leave the freezer paper on while sewing or take it off.

Removing the templates means you'll be stitching in traditional needle-turn mode, with no marked line. You'll develop an appliquér's sense of the right amount to turn under. This is very pleasant stitching, my favorite way to work. However, I do sometimes leave the freezer paper on when I feel the need for extra control over placement and shape.

Note: If you prefer a marked line, you can trace around the templates before removing them.

Stitching with the freezer paper on facilitates precise, flat work. The edge of the paper provides a crisp, identifiable turning line. The stitching technique is the same, though you'll need to tip the sewing line up towards you slightly to avoid sewing through the paper. In some instances the paper actually gets in the way. When this happens, you can fold a portion of the paper back, stitch the area, then replace the paper. I often stitch star points this way. You can also tear away a section of the template or remove the whole thing part-way through if you no longer need it.

Positioning the motif

Stems, vines, and straight strips are positioned along the previously marked lines on the background fabric (see "Fabric preparation" on page 25). Be sure to leave a generous extra length at each end. You can easily trim off what you don't need later.

Other motifs: Place the motif on the background near where you think it might go. Lay the placement guide on top and align the center marks on all four sides with the marks or creases on the background. Without shifting the placement guide, reach underneath and nudge the motif into place. If the template is on, it will line up exactly with the traced shape. If the template has been removed, adjust the motif until an equal amount of margin is visible all the way around (except for the extra amounts in areas that will be overlapped). Lay the guide back down, re-check the centering marks, and re-check the motif. When all is satisfactory, remove the guide and, without shifting the piece, baste it in place. You can baste right through freezer paper.

Securing the motif

For stems, vines, and straight strips, I've come to find that glue can be my friend. A little dab of glue stick works well to secure these elements in place for stitching. Or, you can apply fusible after the strips are made, then fuse them in place.

Other motifs: Many accomplished appliqué artists pin them in place while stitching. I find more satisfactory results through basting with needle and thread. It only takes a few seconds to baste each motif in place, then there are no pins to contend with, and the interior of the motif isn't raised up. Baste fairly close to all stitching edges. Then, when the project is folded or rolled to get a proper grip on it, the edges of the motif will not be able to shift.

Basting can sometimes cause appliqué needles to bend, so I often keep a second-tier needle handy for basting. No. 10 straw needles are good basting needles.

Holding the project

When stitching, hold your work from the bottom in your non-sewing hand. This hand should always stay in a neutral position, without bending or twisting the wrist. Fold or roll the project until you can get a good over-and-under grip on the section you're working on, just ahead of where you're stitching. Your thumb is on top and your fingers are underneath. They hold the background and the turned edge of the motif just ahead of where you are placing your stitch.

Adjust your fold/roll/grip as often as necessary to get proper access and angle for your stitching.

Don't let go with your gripping hand. Use your sewing hand to work with the appliqué pieces.

Supporting the project

Support your work. Holding the project up in midair allows the background fabric to fall away from your hands, which encourages buckling of the appliqué pieces. Use a footstool and sew in your lap, not up close to your face if you can help it. If you need better light or better glasses, gentle quilter, I encourage you to seek ways in which to improve these situations.

The 12" quilter's pressing/cutting mat is an excellent appliqué aid. The hard side serves as a basting surface and the cushioned side supports your hand and the project comfortably while stitching.

Preparing to stitch

Load your needle with fine thread, not too long, and put a small, tight knot in the end.

Choose the area where you will begin stitching. Motifs that stand alone can be started anywhere, but it is usually best to start on the straightest part. Circles... start anywhere! More about circles later. If the motif is to be overlapped, begin at the point where it first emerges. Leave the overlapped margin unsewn so that you can trim it later if need be.

Right-handed stitchers will sew counterclockwise and left-handers will sew clockwise. Fold or roll the project and get a good grip on the selected area with your non-sewing hand (wrist in a neutral position).

"Needle-turn" appliqué means just that—the margin is turned under with the tip of the needle. I call my personal variation "finger pinch, needle poke." While holding the needle temporarily in my curled-up second finger, I use forefinger and thumb to tuck and pinch the margin under, less than ½" ahead of where I am stitching. I also use the needle sometimes to make small refinements to the stitching edge.

Try using the needle and try tucking with the finger. Your technique will end up being the one you are most comfortable with and that gives you results you like. A note about needle-turn: Using the needle tends to draw the margin back towards you. Take care not to create a bump in a curve that should be smooth. Finger-tucking tends to chase the margin forward, which for me avoids creating bumpy curves.

Stitching

Create the first ½" of folded margin and hold it with your gripping hand. Some appliquérs bring the needle up inside the fold. I usually start my thread in the back, bringing my needle up through the background fabric. This first stitch catches a couple of threads of the fold.

Where do you place your needle tip for the next stitch? You won't really be able to see it, but visualize going back in exactly where you just came out. Avoiding the motif edge, insert the needle tip into the background fabric only, just where the current stitch came out.

Push the needle tip forward just slightly, traveling underneath the background fabric. Come back up through the background a very small distance ahead and catch a couple threads of the fold.

"Sink" your stitches. As you pull up the thread after each stitch, give it a gentle hint of a tug. Not so much as to pull up or pucker the piece, just enough to make the stitch sink into the fabric edge.

As you complete a stitch, it helps to pull the thread out at a right angle to the edge of the motif. This helps you gauge exactly where the last stitch came out. Stitches that are placed ahead or behind will be angled stitches, which are longer and more conspicuous.

Each stitch is taken and pulled up individually. There is no modern shortcut in hand appliqué. Speed increases with experience and confidence.

Tying off the thread

On the final stitch, insert the needle through the background and pull it all the way through to the back. Turn the block over. Right next to the thread, take a tiny tack beneath the motif and slowly pull the loop down. Before the loop is closed, put the needle through it, then snug the loop down. Make another tack if you like, but I decided awhile ago that I would save days and years of my life by only doing one. Bury the thread tail by running the needle between the background and the motif before cutting off.

It's the tip

However you sew, by hand or machine, appliquéing or piecing, remember that it's what the tip of the needle is doing that's important. The rest of the needle just follows.

Points

Sew to within two or three stitches of the point. Trim off the folded-under puppydog ear that is sticking out on the other side of the point.

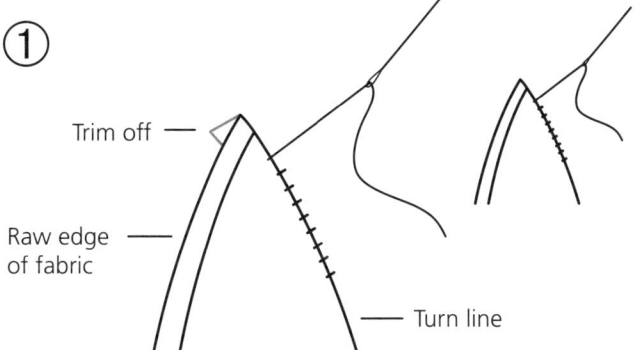

Fold the tip down square across.

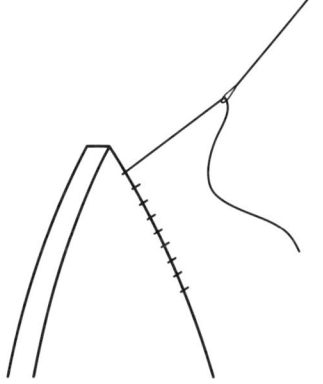

Take the remaining stitches to the point, the last one coming right out of the tip.

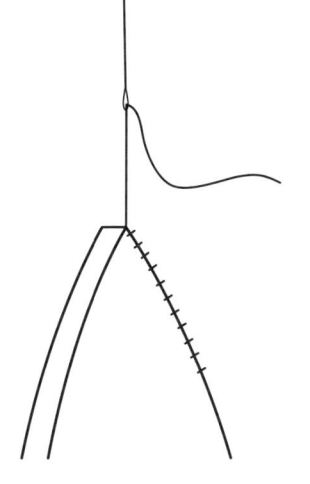

Turn the project.

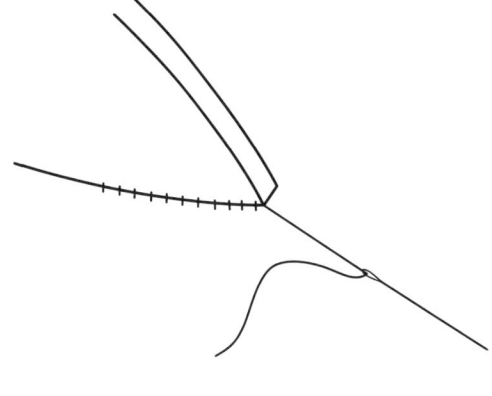

Starting at the point, tuck the margin under. Don't try to start further up and then work down to the point. There will be no room for it. Work from the very point upwards. Chasing the turned margin uphill helps.

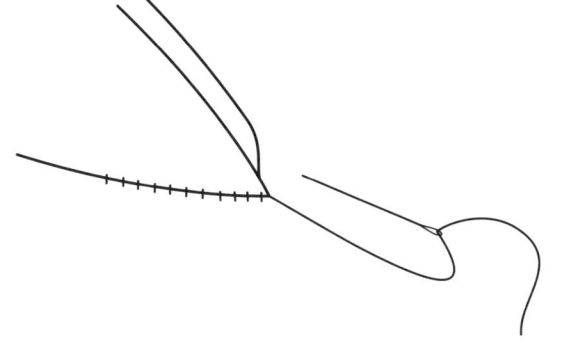

When all is arranged satisfactorily, continue to stitch.

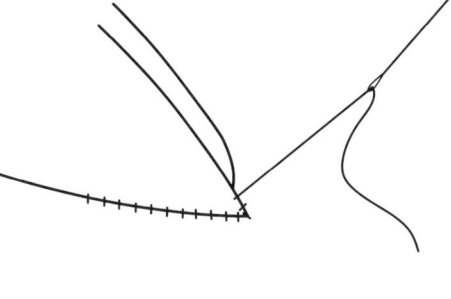

Notches

Clip almost to the turn line.

① Raw edge of fabric — Turn line

Sew to within two or three stitches of the notch. There will be very little margin in this area. That's okay. Use very small stitches and tuck under any loose threads.

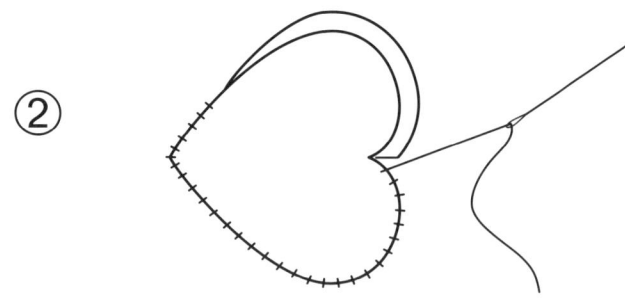

②

Turn the project. Tuck under the first bit of margin on the other side of the notch. In this illustration, some ornery threads from the motif fabric are sticking up in the notch. The needle is not stitching; it is behind the motif, ready to sweep the loose threads under.

③

Use the shaft of the needle to sweep across the notch, creating a tiny fold and encouraging any threads to go under. The needle is still not stitching, just sweeping.

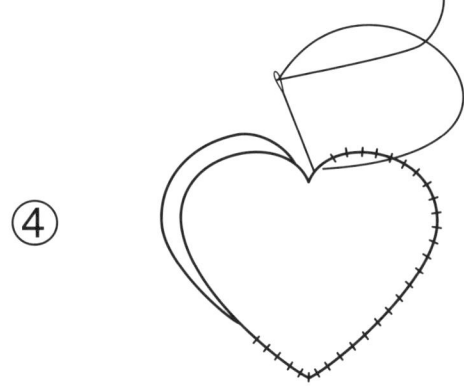

④

Take the remaining stitches down to the notch. The last one, directly in the notch, should pick up three or four threads of the motif fabric.

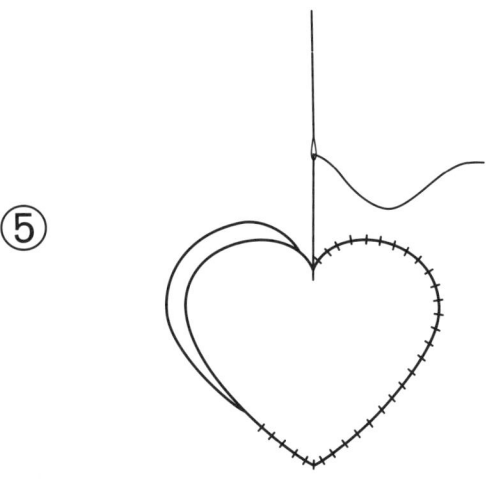

⑤

Sweep again if necessary. With the tip of the needle, dig under the motif fabric and insert the needle exactly where the current stitch came out. Swing the needle and come out going uphill for the next stitch. Snug the thread down well to create a sharp notch.

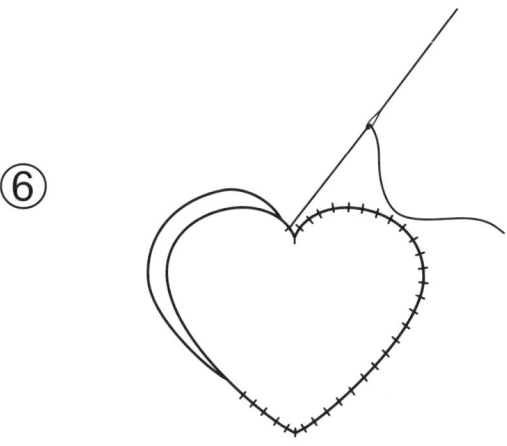

⑥

Building the appliqué block

Continue adding pieces in the order you've assigned. Do not stitch areas that are overlapped by other pieces. If the raw edge to be left unsewn is of any size, you can run your thread behind the background up into the margin and baste across it. This usually occurs at the end of the sewing for the piece. In this case, I skip the tying off process and finish with a backstitch. I don't think the motif is going anywhere.

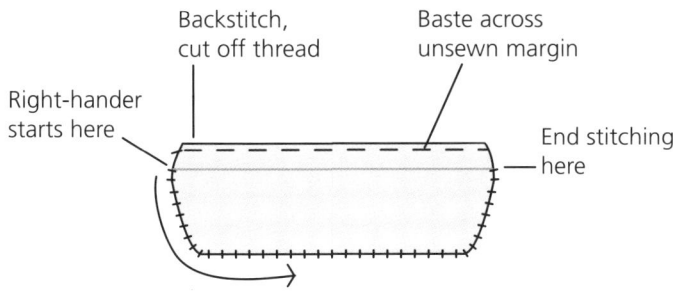

As you complete each piece, remove the main basting thread and the freezer paper if you are using it.

While other forms of "prepared-edge" appliqué allow placement of multiple pieces at a time, I baste and sew one motif at a time, relying on my tissue overlay for accurate placement. You can try placing, basting, and sewing more than one piece. Just be aware that the more the motifs are handled, the more potential for frayed edges and loosened freezer paper.

Circles

There are tools on the market to help make "perfect" circles. Check the gadget section of your favorite quilt shop. There are also low-tech ways. Some appliquérs use a running stitch to gather the circle around a template, then press a crease into it. I usually just appliqué circles like any other shape, chasing the margin forward until the bitter end, when some back-and-forth adjustment of the last little bit of margin is usually necessary to distribute the bulk, resulting in a smooth bumpless curve.

Circles can also be buttons, or yoyos! Consider using these for basket elements or flower centers.

Removing the background

Cutting away the background fabric behind the motifs is a matter of choice, depending on what kind of appearance you prefer and how you plan to quilt the project.

The size of the motif factors into the decision. Small motifs are not practical to cut out behind and should be left alone. Larger motifs present a choice.

Removing the background layer creates a flatter appearance. If you are building up several layers of appliqué, or plan to hand-quilt on top of the motifs, you may decide it's a good idea. When layering, cut out behind each motif as you go. Otherwise, it's best to wait until just before assembling the quilt, as removing portions of the background fabric can somewhat destabilize the blocks. Handle them carefully afterwards.

Leaving the background in place lends a subtle impression of more dimensionality. This is a fine choice if the project will be machine-quilted or if you prefer a less flat look and you don't mind hand-quilting through an extra layer of fabric.

To cut out behind, pull the background layer away from the motif. Pinch a fold in the background and make a nip through it. Keeping the layers separate and taking care not to cut the motif, use scissors to cut away the background fabric. Leave about a scant ¼" inside the stitching line.

The final trim

When all pieces are stitched and any removal of the background fabric is complete, press the block. To encourage the appliqué forward instead of mashing it flat, place a fluffy towel on the ironing board and lay the block face down on it, then press from the back. This can be especially important if your blocks are embellished.

After pressing, trim the block to its unfinished size. Now start another, fellow appliqué enthusiast!

The Particulars

The quilts

All appliqué designs by Kay Mackenzie. Individual projects as noted.

The quilters

Pam Crooks of Soquel, California, is an enthusiastic and prolific appliqué artist. She can never be found without a stitching project or her astounding thread collection. Pam is a member of the Appliqué Goddesses of Silicon Valley.

Janet Locey of San Juan Bautista, California, is an amazing quiltmaker who is skilled at a number of machine techniques. She teaches classes, organizes quilting retreats, designs and publishes patterns, and has her own on-line business featuring Singer Featherweights in addition to nifty quilting supplies. Read all about it at www.henscratchquilting.com.

The quilt puppy

Willie, a seven-pound papillon, is the real quilt puppy. He's a very good quilt dog, keeping Kay company in the studio and approving all of her quilts for the qualities that a dog requires. The only thing Willie does not understand is why he cannot sleep on a quilt while it is being quilted.

The author

Kay Mackenzie caught the quilt pox fourteen years ago and has been working on a quilting project or eight ever since. You are invited to view a gallery of her work at www.quiltpuppy.com. Now Kay combines her love for quilting with her writing and illustrating skills in Quilt Puppy Publications & Designs.

Kay lives with her husband, science journalist Dana Mackenzie, Willie (the real quilt puppy), and three cats in Santa Cruz, California.

The book

Design, illustrations, and layout by Kay Mackenzie using Adobe® Illustrator®, Photoshop®, and InDesign® on an iMac G5. Title typeface is Bodoni Classic Deco Roman (Wiescher); subtitle and headings are Frivolous (Typadelic). Text is Usherwood (ITC-Adobe); captions are Frutiger (Linotype AC-Adobe).

Photography by Tony Grant, Santa Cruz.

Printed by Community Printers, Santa Cruz; www.comprinters.com.

Kay's other books

A Merry Little Christmas to Appliqué includes happy Christmas-time designs in a variety of shapes and sizes that play nicely together.

Growing Hearts to Appliqué features flowering hearts designs to appliqué using your favorite method.

Teapots to Appliqué presents delightful teapot designs for your appliqué pleasure.

In a Twinkle: Youthful Quilt Designs features five fresh quilts made "in a twinkle" for the little loved ones in your life, plus a comfy cozy flannel blankie. All patterns included, with fully illustrated instructions. Projects are suitable for quilters of all levels.

Dog Cabin: A Fast Fun Theme-Quilt Project helps you use your favorite theme from today's novelty fabrics to make a refreshingly fast, fun, and easy quilt top. **QuiltersReview.com** says, "It's just plain fun to read" and "the instructions are crystal-clear." Suitable for quilters of all levels, and very beginner-friendly.

Ask for these titles at your favorite quilt shop or visit www.quiltpuppy.com.